The Pride in Suffolk's Past Project

The aims of the Pride in Suffolk's Past project are two-fold. Firstly, to explore and share the hidden stories of LGBTQ+ people from Suffolk's past. Equally, it aims to collect contemporary stories of Suffolk's LGBTQ+ Community, documenting people's experiences through a period of monumental societal change towards sexuality and gender identity.

The project was developed after two of our Archive Assistants highlighted that they thought the archive had LGBTQ+ stories yet to be fully discovered. We were aware that the archives held collections relating to people who potentially identified as LGBTQ+, but that their records had not been viewed from the perspective of LGBTQ+ History. Subsequently, we decided to re-visit the contents of our collections in the hope that we would discover hidden histories.

Alongside archival research, we also invited members of Suffolk's present LGBTQ+ community to share their stories with us through our online smartsurvey. Participants could share their personal experiences and opinions about current issues the community faces. This publication additionally features special contributions from local figures who share their thoughts on topics such as the rural experience, Suffolk Pride, and youth work.

This publication is only one part of the overall outcome of the Pride in Suffolk's Past project. An exhibition that takes place from February to April 2021 at the Hold in Ipswich. It features much of the content found in this publication as well as items from our archive and other heritage institutions. The project also facilitated community engagement, talks as part of the Outing the Past festival, and an online display for Pride month.

Trigger Warnings

Some topics and language that are featured in this publication could trigger an emotional reaction or cause offence. Archive content has been presented as it was originally created and may contain outdated cultural depictions or language. These were wrong in the past, and they are wrong today.

Topics: Death penalty, persecution by religious doctrine, colonialism, suicide, HIV and AIDS, violent abuse, abusive language, discrimination, drug use, illness, medical terminology, mental health, offensive language, outdated cultural depictions, racism.

Contents

Introduction by Dr Louise Carter

Dr Louise Carter is a social and cultural historian of Britain and lecturer at the University of Suffolk.

It was a great pleasure to be asked to write an introduction for this publication by the organisers of the Pride in Suffolk's Past project. For as enjoyable as History as entertainment or 'the new cookery' might be, it's vital that we never forget the deeper role that History plays in telling us who we are, where we've been and what matters. To do that effectively and to prevent any part of our community being condemned to "the enormous condescension of posterity" as E.P. Thompson might term it, History must tell all our stories and illuminate all our pasts. Towards this end, waves of recovery history focusing on untold histories of gender, race, class, sexuality, disability, age and beyond have rippled out since the 1960s, restoring once marginalised historical actors to the main stage. The Pride in Suffolk's Past project is a valuable contribution to that mission in both spotlighting the rich diversity of past Suffolk communities and in demonstrating the contemporary importance of actively seeking and uncovering more recent testimonies that might otherwise be lost. As both the historical and contemporary contributions here make plain, the history of the LGBTQ+ community is no more homogenous or linear than any other, containing a wide variety of experiences and perspectives, challenges and joys, peaks and troughs. Factors such as period, sex, class, race, age, politics and religion all played a role in shaping individual histories and degrees of protection or exposure to the worst excesses of discrimination on the basis of sexuality. Put together though, these case studies make plain the collective and individual burdens of navigating legal, occupational, cultural, familial and personal discrimination, and whilst it is encouraging to read so many optimistic contemporary accounts, the collection overall underlines the necessity of protecting and strengthening the rights, recognition and freedoms so recently hard-won from any future incursion or erosion.

I hope this publication will serve a range of purposes. Firstly, that it will provide a useful introduction to the lives of LGBTQ+ individuals living in or connected with Suffolk in the past and that the accompanying commentary will help to place these case studies within the wider national and international context. I hope that some will feel the thrill of reading histories that include people they can personally identify with, perhaps for the first time, and that the deliberate focus on LGBTQ+ individuals as an integral part of Suffolk's collective history might inspire more people to feel that History is for them, about them and speaks to them in a fresh and relevant way. I also hope that this brief survey encourages further research drawing on the archival resources at Suffolk Archives to illuminate more detailed insights into the specific experience of Suffolk. As work in this area increases it will be especially interesting to compare the key national and international events and markers noted here, with any emerging regional and place-specific variations. Finally, I share with the project organisers a hope that the project serves as a launch pad for uncovering and preserving more records that provide insights into LGBTQ+ lives from an ever-wider cross-section of society. The personal stories, official documents and digital, material and visual sources collected today will provide the raw materials for LGBTQ+ historians of the future, so if you have a story to share and want future histories to reflect the full diversity of our community, do consider sharing it!

The Research Process

Researchers have a responsibility to gather and present their findings in an ethical manner. Publicising the content of personal archives has the potential to cause harm if they are not handled with sensitivity. The privacy of historical people and living relatives should be thought through, as well as the emotional reaction of those reading the story today.

Discussing the sexual orientation and gender identity of past people requires great sensitivity. Most of the historical figures featured lived during a time when identifying as LGBTQ+ was considered socially unacceptable or was illegal. This means that we do not have confirmation from these people about how they identified. There may be evidence to suggest this information, but it cannot be stated with certainty. Nevertheless, it is vital not to deny our LGBTQ+ community a sense of shared history.

These ethical concerns have been taken into consideration throughout this project. We wanted this work to bring the stories of LGBTQ+ people to the fore and show that Suffolk has an important LGBTQ+ history that needs to be shared. We also wanted to help build up the shared identity of our LGBTQ+ community today. We intend all material from our research to go towards achieving these aims.

Retrospective outing

It is important to avoid any circumstance where someone's gender or sexual identity could be 'outed' against their will. Many of the individuals featured in this publication are well known public figures whose relationships were not explicitly declared but equally were not concealed from view; therefore suggestions have been offered regarding gender and sexual orientation but avoid making decisive statements.

Language

Care must be taken in the appropriate use of historical vocabulary that could cause offence to any minority group. Suffolk Archives consulted several groups from the LGBTQ+ community before this publication went to print to ensure appropriate and inclusive language was used. However, we cannot completely avoid certain vocabulary from the past. It is important to learn what these words meant in the context of their time and share why they are now unacceptable to use today.

Pronouns and anonymity

Throughout this publication the pronouns which best reflect the identities of the people featured have been used. In the case of Colonel Barker, who lived part of their life as a woman and part as a man, the pronouns they/them have been used as we do not have confirmation as to how they identified. For stories shared through contemporary collecting, we have used the preferred pronouns of those who informed us. If their preferred pronouns were not shared, we have used they/them. Furthermore, everyone who submitted material about themselves to the project were asked in writing to state whether they were happy for their identity and material to be shared publicly with the option to remain anonymous. For those who took part in Oral History recordings, they were given participation and recording agreements on which they could state their preference for anonymity and could request to limit public access for a time frame of their choice.

Acknowledging the silences

The research for Pride in Suffolk's Past has used the Suffolk Archives collection and published materials. It has not always been possible to recognise the full breadth and diversity of LGBTQ+ stories from Suffolk's past within our archival material.

Perceptions of what archive collections should include have changed over time. Previously, the materials collected by an archive have tended focused on people who were wealthy, most likely white, and in positions of power or social influence. Those who were not part of these groups were less likely to be represented in archival material. This perception has changed, and Suffolk Archives now strive to include and uplift the stories of those who were traditionally marginalised.

The LGBTQ+ stories from the Suffolk Archives collections noticeably lack ethnic diversity and we acknowledge that this is due to the marginalisation of Black, Caribbean, African, South Asian, Eastern Asian and South-Eastern Asian people's histories. We know that there were people from these communities who were also part of the Suffolk LGBTQ+ community in the past but finding evidence in local historic records is challenging. Suffolk Archives are striving to ensure our contemporary collecting is reflective of the diversity of Suffolk's LGBTQ+ population to ensure everyone's experiences are recorded for future generations.

The stories of working-class LGBTQ+ people in the past are also underrepresented in our collections. In the past working-class people were less likely to have their experiences recorded or shared with an archive. Many working-class LGBTQ+ stories were only recorded in relation to criminality. Criminal records such as the local Assizes show the names and occupations of LGBTQ+ people who had been persecuted for their sexuality or gender. However, we do not get a sense of who they were as people in the same way that we can build up an understanding of those who were of a higher social standing.

The Act was passed during the reign of King Henry VIII and moved the matter of 'sodomy' from the ecclesiastical courts to the state.

The Act did not explicitly target same-sex acts between men as it also applied to acts between men and women. However, it was male same-sex convictions that were by far the most common and publicised. Convictions under the 'Buggery Act' were punishable by death.

On 27th March 1790, John Southwell and John Smith were charged with 'sodomy' at the Bury Assizes. It is recorded that the act took place at an 'Army Camp' and tells us that Southwell used to be the postmaster for Saxmundham. Both men were sentenced to hanging at Rushmere on 3rd April.

The Farce of Sodom

One of the oldest documents relating to LGBTQ+ history in Suffolk Archives is a copy of the play 'The Farce of Sodom'. The manuscript dates to 1694 and is presumed to be by John Wilmot, the Earl of Rochester. There are only ten known surviving copies.

The story is believed to be a satirical interpretation of the royal court of King Charles II. The main character, King Bolloxian of Sodom, decrees that 'sodomy' be the sole acceptable sexual practice and as a result his kingdom descends into chaos. This is thought to be a reaction to King Charles' willingness to tolerate Catholicism through the Royal Declaration of Indulgence.

The play is considered to be a piece of erotic literature. The characters' names are crude 'play on words' of old English sexual slang and profanities.

Although it is notable that same-sex intercourse is explored openly in the play, the king's advocation for 'sodomy' is ultimately portrayed as being absurd and dangerous. There are clear differences in the way acts between same-sex and different-sex people are staged. Intercourse between men and women is acted out on stage for the audience to see but intercourse between men is not explicitly shown.

The 'Buggery Act' was repealed and replaced by the Offences Against the Person Act 1828. The new language of the law focused on male same-sex activity explicitly, where the 'Buggery Act' had applied to men and women collectively. Same-sex acts between men remained punishable by death.

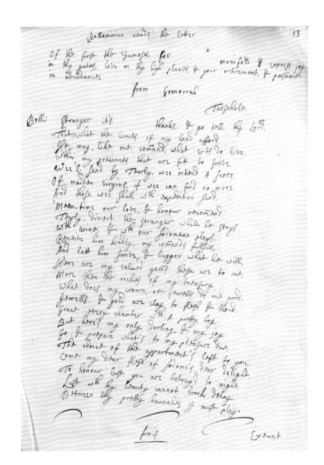

The last page of a manuscript of the 'Farce of Soddom', c.1684. 194/6/1

What do the terms 'sodomy' and 'buggery' mean?

Sodom was a Biblical city featured in the book of Genesis. Along with the city of Gomorrah, Sodom was destroyed by fire and brimstone sent from God for the wicked sins of the men who lived in the cities. What exactly their sins were is the subject of debate, but it was traditionally interpreted to be sexual promiscuity, particularly of a male same-sex nature. From this interpretation the concept of 'sodomy' came to mean the act of sexual intercourse between men.

'Buggery' derives from the old French word for heresy. The first known use of the word in connection with the act of 'sodomy' is in the 1533 'Buggery Act'. As the law regarding same-sex relations changed over time, the term 'buggery' was consistently used to describe sexual intercourse between men and was part of legal vocabulary in Britain until 2004.

Both words are unacceptable terms to describe same-sex intercourse in a modern-day context due to their links to criminality and societal oppression.

&Edward Fitzgerald
Joseph Fletcher

Edward Fitzgerald (1809-1883) was a poet, writer and translator born in the Suffolk village of Bredfield who attended King Edward VI School in Bury St Edmunds. He is widely known for his translation of The Rubaiyat of Omar Khayyam, a collection of poems written by the great Persian philosopher, Omar Khayyam.

Although he was married to the daughter of a fellow poet, Edward developed a loving relationship with a young man named Kentworthy Browne. He admired Browne with intensity, comparing their relationship with the biblical story of David and Jonathan where 'Jonathan became one in spirit with David, and loved him as himself'. Unfortunately, Browne died suddenly in a riding accident and Fitzgerald was left with a 'vacant place in [his] heart'.

Photograph of Posh Fletcher. 1300/72/19/26

The last two men to be executed for 'buggery' were James Pratt and John Smith on 27th November 1835.

John Newton from Brandon was charged for 'an unnatural offence' in 1855. He was initially sentenced to death, but it was recommended that his life be spared. He was transported for life to Western Australia in 1857. Many of those convicted of 'buggery' received similar sentences. The death penalty had not yet been abolished but was gradually used less.

Shortly afterwards, Fitzgerald met Joseph Fletcher (otherwise known as 'Posh'), a Suffolk fisherman. Fitzgerald was impressed by Fletcher's physique and character, describing him as 'very much more ladylike than ladies' as well as granting him the title of 'the greatest man' he had ever met.

The two men owned a herring boat together that Fitzgerald called the Meum and Tuum. They enjoyed sailing and drinking together at pubs on the Suffolk coast. Fitzgerald even commissioned a portrait of Posh to be hung in his home. Their relationship ended, however, on bad terms when Posh failed to pay his debts to Fitzgerald and their trust was broken.

It is not clear as to whether Fitzgerald himself identified as being a gay man, even though he would probably be described as such in our modern understanding. It has been suggested that Fitzgerald was not aware of his sexuality and potentially did not identify as being gay. The frank and open way Fitzgerald praises both Posh and Browne in his letters could indicate that he was unaware his feelings were potentially dangerous to express. On the other hand, Fitzgerald may have boldly expressed his sexuality in a way that seems astounding for someone living in the 1800s.

Portrait of Edward Fitzgerald, 1883. 1300/72/35/149

Self-Identity and Labels
Zelly Lisanework

Zelly is a British Ethiopian writer, performance artist, poet, and human rights activist based in Suffolk.

Labels and acronyms have always had a complicated relationship with marginalised identities. There is struggle between acknowledging the intersectional issues that face a community through collective labelling and the individuals within those communities that either embrace or reject labels. The question with labels and acronyms is about who assigned them and what intention and purpose is behind that.

As someone who identifies as a queer black woman, there is a difference between how I feel about the labels I've assigned to myself and the labels assigned to me by others. A part of my identity is within the ever evolving LGBTQIA+ community and while I understand there are reasons behind the assigning of a collective identity, I personally would not identify myself by that acronym as it limits and in some situations erases my identity as an individual.

There has been much discussion around the term BAME, another collective term for people of non-white heritage and its one that I am against using. The M in BAME stands for "Minority" and it's a term assigned by white people which is othering and inaccurate about the Black, Indigenous, African, Caribbean, South Asian, South East Asian and East Asian communities. Ask me who I am and you will know without assumptions that I am a Black woman, a Black British woman but I would be more specific and depending on context, then I would also say one of the following:

I am of British Ethiopian heritage

I am of East African and Ethiopian decent

I am East African and Ethiopian diaspora

Labels can be empowering and comforting, they can also be restrictive and harmful. The word Queer has historically had negative connotations from being weaponised by CISHet people, my choice to identify as a Queer is a political one. I used to identify under singular labels like Gay and Lesbian, but they didn't feel right. For me, Queer is a reclaimed umbrella term that rebels against singular labels, a label without labels which fits my identity more authentically.

We have the right to define our cultural, gender and sexual identities on our own terms instead of having acronyms and labels imposed on us by those who do not identify with our experiences.

Nina Layard & Mary Outram

Nina Frances Layard (1853-1935) was an archaeologist, prehistorian, and poet. In 1898 she worked on the Blackfriars site from 1902 to 1905 and she conducted excavations on Foxhall Road, Ipswich.

At the time, archaeology was a male-dominated field, but Layard was a remarkable exception. She was one of the first women to be admitted to the Society of Antiquaries of London and was the first female president of the Prehistoric Society of East Anglia. Layard worked closely with Ipswich Museum and donated many of her finds to their collections.

In the 1901 census, Layard was living with Mary F Outram who was recorded as a boarder in the house. Both women were described as 'living on independent means'. From then on, the pair lived in various locations together, travelling for the excavations they worked on. Outram assisted Layard's archaeological excavations, often illustrating and transcribing much of Layard's work.

Their mutual respect and admiration for one another could also be found in a personal bond. Neither married, and they lived and worked together for the rest of their lives and are buried in the same grave in Kelvedon churchyard. It is therefore widely understood that the pair were in a same-sex relationship.

Due to contemporary social attitudes and legal persecution, Layard and Outram did not have the opportunity to live openly as a lesbian couple, but their decision to spend their lives together as well as pursuing careers in the archaeological field is a testament of their courage.

Photograph of Nina Layard on an excavation at Valley Road brick works, Ipswich. S2/3/1.1

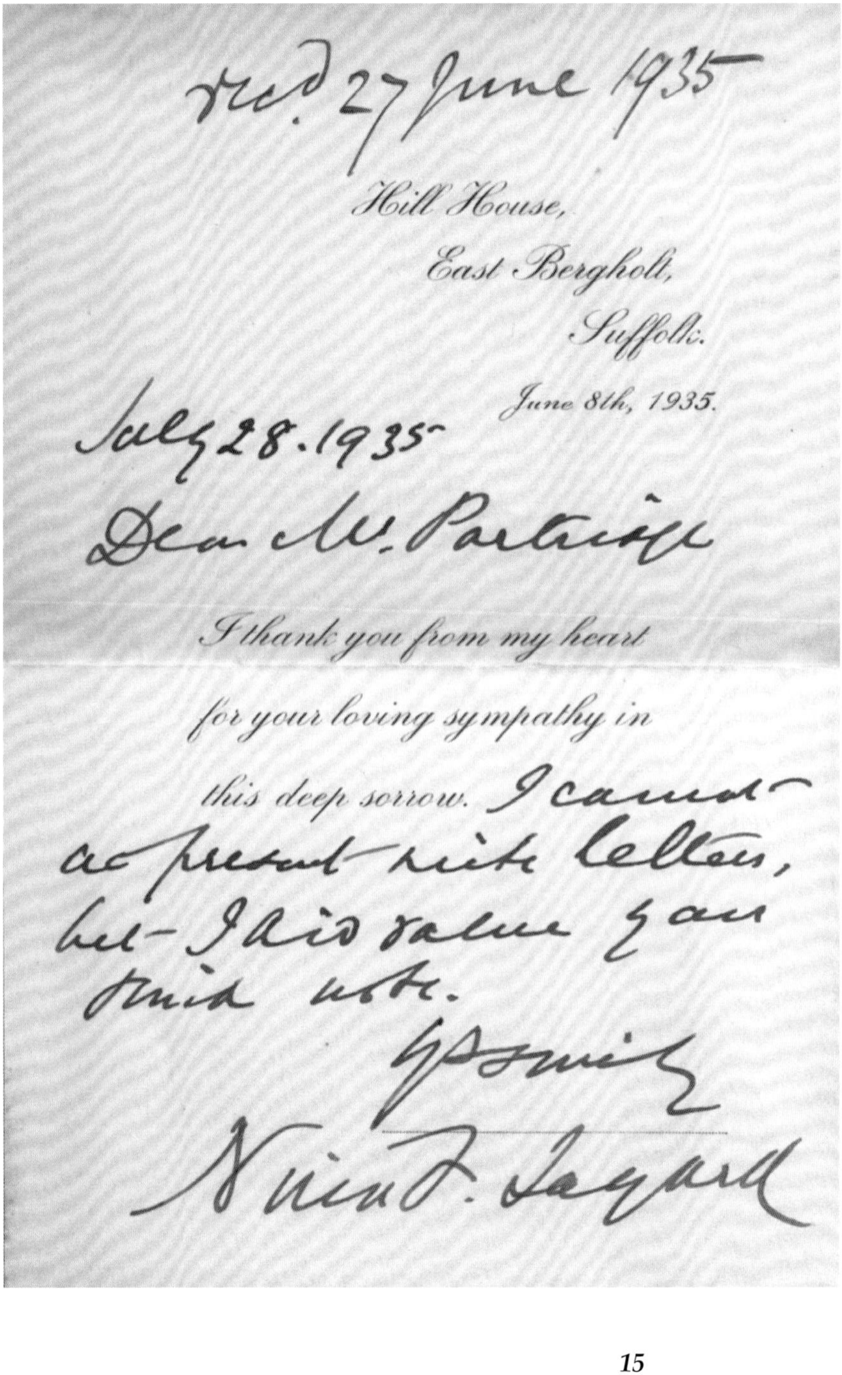

rec.d 27 June 1935

Hill House,
East Bergholt,
Suffolk.

June 8th, 1935.

July 28. 1935

Dear Mr. Partridge

I thank you from my heart

for your loving sympathy in

this deep sorrow. I cannot

at present write letters,

but I did value your

kind note.

Yrs sincerely

Nina F. Layard

Note from Nina Layard to thank Charles Partridge for his condolences on the death of Mary Outram, 1935. 821.8 LAY

*Photograph of MR James
in the grounds at Shrubland
Hall. c.1914. HA93/SA/3/8/3*

1861 Offences Against the Person Act

This legislation replaced the Offences Against the Person Act 1828, revoking the death penalty for same-sex acts between men and replacing it with a prison term of hard labour between 10 years and life.

1866 Hyde v. Hyde and Woodmansee

Following the court case of Hyde v. Hyde and Woodmansee about a polygamous marriage, (being married to more than one person at the same time) the legal definition of marriage was set as being between one man and one woman. The ruling would have lasting implications for arguments for marriage equality over 100 years later.

M.R. James

Montague Rhodes James (1862-1936) was an academic in Medieval and Bible studies but is best remembered for his ghost stories. Born in Goodnestone, Kent his family moved to The Rectory in Great Livermere, Suffolk in 1865.

In 1893 he became the Director of the Fitzwilliam Museum in Cambridge. James was responsible for cataloguing some of the manuscript collections in the college libraries which led to the 1902 excavation at Bury St Edmunds Abbey. His ghost stories were originally written as entertainment for his friends but were eventually published in several collections. His distinctive style led to the coining of the 'Jamesian' style of ghost storytelling. His stories have been dramatized on television and in radio productions.

James did not marry, although there was pressure on him to find a wife. He was close to his friend and former pupil, James McBryde. McBryde was the illustrator for James' books and they travelled to Demark and Sweden together. McBryde died in 1904 when he was working on the illustrations for James's Ghost Stories of an Antiquary. James maintained a friendship with McBryde's wife and became the legal guardian to his daughter, Jane. It is thought that McBryde was the love of James's life.

Catherine Hilda Duleep Singh

Catherine Hilda Duleep Singh (1871-1942) was a suffragist and the second daughter of the Maharaja Duleep Singh, who had been exiled to Britain after the Anglo-Sikh War. The family lived in Elveden Hall in Suffolk.

Princess Catherine Duleep Singh with Lina Schaffer, 1938. Courtesy of Peter Bance.

Duleep Singh and her sisters were debutantes at Buckingham Palace in 1895, marking their entry into high society. She was a member of the National Union of Women's Suffrage Societies (NUWSS), pursuing a much less militant approach to the suffrage movement than her sister, Sophia.

She had a life-long relationship with Fraulein Lina Schafer who was originally her governess as a young girl. Their affection for one another grew over time and the pair lived together for the rest of their lives. In 1904 Duleep Singh and Schafer moved to Kassel in Germany.

Catherine helped many Jewish families escape from Germany when the Nazis came into power, some even being housed in Duleep Singh's home in England. Schafer died in 1938 and despite her desire to stay in the house in Kassel, Duleep Singh fled from Nazi Germany. When she died in 1942, she requested in her will that a quarter of her ashes be buried as near as possible to Schafer's grave.

Sophia Duleep Singh described their relationship as an 'intimate' one and in 1997 an account and deposit box was discovered which was jointly owned by Catherine Duleep Singh and Lina Schafer, indicating their commitment as a couple.

Photograph of the interior of Elvedon Hall. K505/2481. Reproduced with kind permission of Bury Past and Present Society.

Pride in Suffolk's Past Collecting Survey.

Alongside stories from the past, Suffolk Archives has been collecting experiences of Suffolk's LGBTQ+ community today through an online survey.

An anonymous story

An anonymous contributor shared their experience as a lesbian living in Suffolk with their wife and family as well as their relationship with religion.

‘Other than the very, very occasional stare or tut when I'm holding hands with my wife in public, I have not been personally targeted due to my sexuality. The only area in which I am acutely aware of prejudice is, sadly, from religious institutions. My wife was excommunicated from her church because of her relationship with me. We now attend a different denomination and have been completely accepted and embraced as a family by our small village congregation.

The legalisation of gay marriage in 2014 has also, of course, been a huge change and one that has allowed my wife and I, along with so many others, to feel that our relationship is respected and validated on an equal footing to other married couples.'

Georgia's story

Georgia was born and raised in Ipswich. She identifies as lesbian and in 2019 she contributed to Suffolk Pride by creating artwork to promote the parade. She shared her thoughts with us about current societal attitudes regarding LGBTQ+ people.

'I feel like LGBTQ+ people are much more accepted now, and much less the butt of jokes, than we were in the 90s.

Of course, there are some circles and ideologies within which we are a topic of scorn and derision, but these are much less generally socially acceptable - at least in the UK.

…I also notice that younger generations are much more open about their sexualities and seem much more comfortable to publicly and proudly present as LGBTQ+. And this fills me with pride and hope.'

Despite these positive steps in the right direction, Georgia expressed her sadness that a lot more needs to be done both locally and around the world:

'Closer to home, I still feel a level of fear when holding my girlfriend's hand in the town centre. Whenever I wear an item depicting rainbow colours, I wonder if it will attract negative attention.

LGBTQ+ people are still widely discriminated against - elsewhere in the world, people are still tortured, imprisoned, or killed for being LGBTQ+.'

Pride artwork created by Georgia Goddard. 2019.
www.georgiagoddard.com

Charles Partridge

Charles Partridge (1872-1955) was a genealogist, anthropologist, local historian and colonial officer born in the village of Offton, Suffolk. He lived in Stowmarket as a child and attended The Queen Elizabeth School in Ipswich.

During his lifetime, Partridge collected artefacts, photographs, books and papers, one of his most notable collections being his work on the histories and pedigrees of Suffolk families.

He had a close association with Lillian Redstone, Archivist at Ipswich and East Suffolk Record Office, who frequently worked with him. There are also letters from Nina Layard regarding her ancestry within this collection.

Amongst these records, there are letters and photographs from fellow officers and men he had met throughout his career in both the colonial service and in the army during the First World War. Some of the letters he received tell of the intense relationships he had with these men.

On 1st December 1916, a Private in the Royal Army Service Corps wrote an impassioned letter to Partridge:

'I shall never forget you as I cannot and I shall not get settled at this life until I am with you.
If it cannot be done, I want to be with you after the war and then to spend the rest of my life with you, as sir there is no man on the face of the earth that I want to be with more then you, as, if I may say so, I right down love you as you were so kind to me.'

Pte F Welham 268886
Bromley Kent
Dec 1st 1916

Dear Sir

In answer to your nice letter
which I was so pleased to receive this
morning hope to find you in best of
health as I am fine you see I am in the
suit at last & this is a fine life
my luck I have got into the M.T. at S.6
and also passed my test I am on a Ford
car & you should should see me some
soldier

how I am writing to ask you if you can
get me to Salonika with you as I am
always thinking of the grand time we
had when you were at home

You said in your letter came I remember
when we were at Bury I shall never
forget you as I can not & I shall not
get settled at this life until I am with
you if it cannot be done I want to be
with you after the war & then wish
to spend the rest of my life with you
as Sir there is no man on the face
of the earth that I want to be with

During his colonial service, Partridge was stationed in Nigeria and governed over the indigenous people from the Cross River region. His role in the colonial system and his personal actions have to be carefully considered. His personal attitude was unusual in that Partridge made some efforts to understand the indigenous Cross River people and prevented the theft of important cultural material. Nevertheless, Partridge was an important figure in an oppressive system that exploited the people and resources of many countries around the world. His position as a colonial officer gave him illegitimate authority to enforce colonial boundaries, labour schemes, and punishment on to the indigenous people.

*Letter from Private
F Welham to Charles
Partridge dated
1st December 1916.
HA126/329/3*

Dr Louisa Garrett Anderson & Dr Flora Murray

Louisa Garrett Anderson (1873-1943) was a surgeon and suffragette. Although she was born in London, her family lived in Aldeburgh, Suffolk. Her mother, Elizabeth Garrett Anderson, was the first woman to qualify as a doctor in Britain. She carried on her mother's legacy through her medical career.

When war broke out in 1914, Louisa Garret Anderson founded the Women's Hospital Corps, which served overseas in France. The military hospital treated wounded soldiers and was staffed entirely by women. Garrett Anderson performed nearly 7,000 operations. The staff were eventually invited to run Endell Street Military Hospital in London.

Despite her significant contributions to the suffrage movement and the advancement of women, Louisa's name is rarely mentioned in history. Her absence may be linked to the fact that she shared her life with another woman: Dr Flora Murray.

Flora Murray (1869-1923) was the personal physician for Emmeline Pankhurst. She treated the women who had been force-fed whilst in prison for taking part in militant protests for women's suffrage. She also jointly opened the Women's Hospital for Children and the Women' Hospital Corps with Garrett Anderson.

Although we are unable to know for certain whether they both

Louisa Garrett Anderson outside Endell Street Hospital with her two dogs, c.1918. HA436/4/1/12

identified as lesbians, their actions suggest that they were in a relationship. The two women lived together and are buried together under the words 'we have been gloriously happy'.

Amanda Markwell, Archive Assistant at Suffolk Archives, has explored the nature of their relationship within both her undergraduate dissertation and her MRes thesis. Originally, this research concluded that both women had been marginalised from historical narratives because of their sexuality but this marginalisation is beginning to change. New documents have recently come to light and works about their experiences during the war have been published.

She also suggests that the pair's relationship marks a strong link between the feminist ideals of the suffrage movement and second wave feminism. The idea that lesbianism shapes personal self-determination and commitment to women was a key concept for many second-wave feminists but Garrett Anderson and Murray demonstrate this concept much earlier.

Flora Murray at her desk in Claridge's, Paris. Courtesy of The Women's Library at LSE.

'Having access to your own history is important. Knowledge of the past gives us a context in which to place ourselves. It also gives us a basis for our efforts to change and reassess things.'

-Amanda Markwell

As part of the Criminal Law Amendment Act 1885, Section 11 was used to prosecute those who committed 'any acts of gross indecency with male persons'.

In addition, the Act changed the terms of punishment - the minimum term of hard labour was reduced to two years. The amendment was used to prosecute Oscar Wilde in 1895, who was sent to prison and given two years' hard labour.

Colonel Barker

Colonel Victor Barker (1895-1960) lived an extraordinary life. Assigned female at birth, they initially seemed to align themself to traditional gender norms, becoming a nurse and joining the Women's Auxiliary Air Force.

In 1923 they left their partner Earnest Pearce-Crouch due to his drinking and violent behaviour and assumed the identity of Colonel Victor Barker. Presenting as a man, Barker began a relationship with Elfrida Haward and they were married in Brighton in 1923.

Barker was taken to Brixton prison in 1929 when they were charged with perjury. Whilst at Brixton, their assigned sex of female was revealed, and they were transferred to Holloway Prison

Illustrations of Colonel Barker of the front cover of The Graphic, 16th March 1929.
*© Illustrated London News/Mary Evans Picture Library.**

for Women. Instead of perjury, Barker was eventually convicted of making a false statement on their marriage certificate.

After their prison sentence, Barker performed in a peep show with Haward at Blackpool Marquee. Barker and Haward drew crowds to Blackpool who came to watch the couple lie next to each other in single beds.

Barker was also known for their association with the British Union of Fascists. They were a member of the British National Fascists and trained young recruits in boxing.

After the Second World War Barker assumed the new identity of Geoffrey Norton and married Eva Norton by 1956. They lived at 3 Wrights Cottages in Kessingland, Suffolk.

By 1960 Barker was admitted to Lowestoft Hospital before dying on the 18th February, aged 64. It was not until three months after their death that it was revealed Geoffrey Norton was in fact the famous Colonel Barker.

A Lowestoft Journal article from 1960 reports that Barker said they would 'have a better chance of earning a living as a man' and supposedly said they 'simply had to become a man' in order to use their knowledge of horses and farm work. This suggests that the perceptions of male privilege and the opportunities that came with it could have played a role in Barker's identity as a man.

It would be unfair, however, not to consider Colonel Barker's male presentation as a reflection of their gender identity. Their story is one of great importance to trans history as it tells of a gender non-conforming person pursuing ambitious careers (such as a restaurant proprietor and antiques business owner) as well as forming relationships with people of their choosing. On the other hand, their life also highlights just how dangerous it was to live as a trans person, needing to frequently change name and profession to avoid detection.

Darragh's story

Darragh is currently studying at the University of Suffolk and is the university's LGBTQ+ Officer for 2020/2021 academic year.

'I was the university rep at the NUS liberation conference. In addition to this, as a trans man, I have spoken at conferences and events about being transgender and a teenager, and how access to healthcare has affected my life…My coming out predates Stonewall supporting transgender individuals, so I have watched the community grow and become more accepted, and have also watched as the media has tried to fight back - I find it exceptionally inspiring to see our community fighting for equal rights despite the power behind our oppressors.

I originally came out via Facebook in 2014 when I was 13 years old. I came out because a trans guy had come to present at our school during LGBTQ+ week, and I had played around with my labels internally for a few years (liberal access to the internet definitely helped my self-discovery). I was definitely lucky as my parents were actively supportive and immediately tried to get access to resources to make my life easier, although at the time they were definitely lacking in comparison to what is available now.

I have experienced a lot of indirect discrimination through the schooling system. For example, I was actively placed with the girls on school trips despite the fact that I am a boy, and was not allowed to change in the boys' or girls' room (I had to use the disabled toilet) because I might offend other students. These small things build up a narrative inside your head that makes you doubt yourself and think of yourself as another rather than as a person.'

28

Ann's story

Ann has lived in Suffolk for over 40 years. She shared her moving story that gives an insight into how different life was for LGBTQ+ people living in the mid-20th century.

'I was in the Women's Royal Naval Service at the time [of coming out] and went through an investigation process that ended in me being dismissed, hence I had to come out to family quickly. My parents told me to come home but we never really talked about my gayness. I had been in the navy for nearly nine years so had no recent connections in Suffolk. My mother referred me to a colleague who happened to be gay and life started taking off.

I worked for the NHS at a local psychiatric hospital and met some gay women but wasn't out, I knew instinctively that coming out at work was not an option…I left the NHS job and worked for local social services and was amazed at the difference in culture and acceptance of being gay, so was able to be out with colleagues and staff. For the first time in my life I could be me, although still careful in certain situations.

Unfortunately, I couldn't be out in my last relationship as my partner was too worried about her family knowing about our relationship. We were together for 27 and a half years before she died in 2014. For the last 6 months we lived together but still kept up the façade of being friends!

As an older gay woman, it has been difficult to have the confidence to join gay groups having been outside that group for so long. Once I took that first step, I found the groups I've joined very welcoming and supportive. Last year I joined the Pride march in Ipswich with the women's group - my first ever - and was amazed at how friendly it all was.'

Dr William Crowther & Paul Kuehn

Dr William Crowther (1887-1972) was a village doctor for Cavendish, near Sudbury. In December 1947, he was arrested with a German Prisoner of War, Paul Kuehn, who was living at the Prisoner of War (POW) camp on Hardwick Heath in Bury St Edmunds.

A policeman found the two men in the back seat of Crowther's car on a country lane near Whepstead. He did not accept their explanation that they had met for a language lesson and arrested them. Dr Crowther said he did not take Kuehn back to his house as it was 13 miles away and his housekeeper was anti-German. Both were tried for gross indecency.

They denied all charges, and 104 of Crowther's patients signed a petition vouching for his good character. Despite this intervention, both men were found guilty. Kuehn was sentenced to six months in prison. Crowther was bound over for two years on condition he have no more contact with German POWs. He had already sold his medical practice and moved away from the village.

The decision to grant Dr Crowther clemency but sentence Kuehn to six months in prison makes us question whether social standing influenced the leniency of punishment. The judge said to Dr Crowther 'I think the consequences will be most disastrous and I don't propose to add to that punishment by sending a man of your education and ability to prison', suggesting that his class and reputation of respectability prevented him from receiving a harsher sentence.

A CASE WHICH PUZZLED THE JURY

VILLAGERS' PETITION FOR DOCTOR FACING SERIOUS CHARGE

A SENTENCE of six months' imprisonment was passed on Gefr Paul Kuehn, a 45-years-old German P.O.W. at Hardwick Camp, Bury St. Edmunds, after he had pleaded not guilty at the West Suffolk Quarter Sessions on Tuesday, to a charge of committing an act of gross indecency with Dr. William Edmund Crowther, of Cavendish.

Mr. H. E. R. Boileau, prosecuted.

The case was based on the evidence of P.-s. A. Gillings, who related how he came upon a stationary car in Rede Road, Whepstead. Inside was Dr. Crowther and the German prisoner-of-war. When told by witness what he suspected, both denied the offence.

Mr. Robert Ives, defended and Kuehn, speaking through an interpreter, stated that he had been a P.O.W. for over three years, working on farms in England. His home was in the Polish occupied part of Germany, and so was unable to go back. He

Call of the Broads

MEMBERS of the Bury St. Edmunds and District Licensed Victuallers' Association will visit the Broads for their outing in July. This was decided at the annual meeting held under the chairmanship of Mr. J. R. G. Blake.

Officers elected for the coming year were: President, Mr. J. H. A. Clarke; Chairman, Mr. Blake; Vice-Chairman, Mr. G. H. Gould; Treasurer, Mr. E. S. Butler; Secretary, Mr. A. S. Mole; and a committee comprising Mrs. H. Codling, Mrs.

Newspaper articles about Dr William Crowther and Paul Kuehn. 20th February 1948 and 9th April 1948. Reproduced by permission of Bury Free Press.

CAVENDISH DOCTOR AND GERMAN PRISONER SENT FOR TRIAL

A POLICE sergeant who, it was alleged, chanced to come upon a stationary car on a country road containing a doctor and a German prisoner-of-war, was the chief witness in Thingoe Magistrates Court at Bury St. Edmunds on Wednesday when Dr. Wm. Edmund Crowther (60), of New House, Cavendish, and Paul Kuehn, Hardwick P.O.W. Camp, were committed for trial.

The doctor, who was defended by Mr. George Pollock, pleaded not guilty to committing an act of gross indecency with the P.O.W., and the latter pleaded not guilty to being a party to the act. Mr. J. N. B. Ashton defended the German.

Mr. V. D. M. Hall prosecuted in both cases, and that in respect of the doctor was heard first.

Police-Sergeant Gillings, of Horringer, said that while motoring about 4.30 p.m. on December 20th, ten minutes

Wants to contact all who served in regiment

So that all past members of the Suffolk Yeomanry may be notified of the activities of their O.C.A., Capt. W. A. Crack, Welfare Officer, is compiling a list of those who served with the Regiment from 1927-1945.

Records are incomplete, and all who have not received recent notifications, or who

In 1921 three MPs attempted to add a clause to a new Criminal Law Amendment Bill (designed to protect children under the age of 16 from indecent assault): 'Any act of gross indecency between female persons shall be a misdemeanour and punishable in the same manner as any such act committed by male persons under section 11 of the Criminal Law Amendment Act 1885'. Despite agreement from speakers that lesbianism was distasteful, both Houses rejected the clause, and ultimately the entire bill. There was concern that legislation would only draw attention to the offence and encourage women to explore their sexuality.

Lady Eve Balfour

Lady Eve Balfour (1898-1990) was a farmer and pioneer in organic growing methods. She was the niece of Prime Minister Arthur Balfour and daughter of the 2nd Earl of Balfour. It was her childhood dream to become a farmer and she went on to be one of the first women to study agriculture at university, attending what is now Reading University.

In 1919, she bought New Bells Farm in Haughley, Suffolk along with her sister Mary with their inheritance. She famously conducted 'The Haughley Experiment' at New Bells Farm in 1939. The experiment compared the results of chemical and organic farming. Balfour hypothesised that farmers relied too heavily on fertilisers and chemicals and believed that a more natural farming method would be better for human health. She later founded the Soil Association which continues to promote sustainable agricultural methods and awards organic certification to produce.

Balfour lived fifty years of her life alongside Kathleen Carnley, a dairy worker. The pair lived together in a cottage in Haughley. Very little is known about the nature of Balfour and Carnley's relationship. We do not know if they were in a romantic relationship or if they identified as lesbian but the length of time they lived together suggests a strong loving bond between the women.

My experiences of Bi-erasure and improving Bi-visibility

An anonymous contribution

A little bit about me: I'm female, 40 years old (at time of writing in), mixed race (White English and Indian) and bisexual. I live in Ipswich and was brought up here. I work in a public sector organisation. I have two small daughters, and a male partner who I've been with for 13 years. But that still doesn't make me straight. So, why do I feel the need to talk about being bisexual? It is an important part of my identity, just as I identify strongly with my gender and race.

S ome people seem to think you have to 'choose' whether to be gay or straight, and that being bisexual doesn't really exist. This is called 'bi-erasure': literally, erasing bi people. How would you feel if you told me you were straight, and I said, "No you're not"? Or if you told me you supported Ipswich Town and I told you that you were really a closet Norwich supporter?! I know it sounds silly, but you would probably be annoyed if you thought I really meant it and kept saying it. If, like me, you are a bi person in a relationship with someone of the other gender, people just assume you're straight, and often it is easier to let them assume that than to correct them and tell them the truth.

Bisexual Pride Flag.
Pink represents being
attracted to people of the
same gender as you. Blue
represents attraction to
a different gender to you.
Purple represents attraction
to two (or more) genders.

It was in 1997, when I was 17 and had left school that I was inspired by Ellen DeGeneres who came out very publicly. I decided I would start telling people more generally about being bi, including my mum. I always knew she would be ok with it. I had to explain what being bisexual meant (!), but, after that, she said, "I don't care who it is as long as they make you happy". I would also find it difficult to tell my Indian relatives, as they weren't even OK with me living with a man I'm not married to! It took much longer to feel comfortable to be out at work, and there are still some situations in which I don't feel I can talk about it.

Often, when I am in LGBT groups and networks, I avoid using pronouns, only in my case it's so I don't reveal that I'm not in a same-sex relationship; so they don't realise that my partner is male and think I shouldn't be there. When there are social events for these networks and gay people bring their partners, I don't feel able to bring mine. I've had to do work within LGBT groups to overcome these prejudices and raise awareness. At work I ran some sessions about bi awareness. I became the chair of our LGBT staff network, which was a first – I felt I was pioneering, since a bi person in an other-sex relationship, who was pregnant at the time, isn't usually who you would think of as representing the LGBT community! I have run workshops, written articles and featured in our staff newsletter.

I want to reassure anyone reading who may be having a hard time that it won't always be like this. And perhaps those of you who know someone who may be having a hard time can think about what you could do to make it a little bit easier for them, to make them feel accepted and included. To future readers: hopefully the world has changed even more for the better. However, I'm sure there will still be issues of social justice and inclusion: how can you challenge yourself, and other people, to do better?! What story will you leave for posterity?

Benjamin Britten & Peter Pears

Benjamin Britten (1913-1976) was one of the greatest British composers of the twentieth century. Born in Lowestoft, his father was a dentist and his mother an amateur musician who taught him how to play piano. Britten was beginning to compose his own music by the age of five. He later won a scholarship to study at the Royal College of Music.

In 1937 Britten met tenor singer, Peter Pears. Pears was born in Surrey and briefly studied music at Oxford University and then at the Royal College of Music. He was eventually awarded a contract to be one of the BBC singers, a small singing ensemble. The friendship between Britten and Pears blossomed over time, with Britten writing his first composition for Pears within weeks of meeting.

The pair sailed to North America together on the eve of the Second World War to evade the hostility for being pacifists. During this time, their relationship evolved into one of a romantic nature. They returned to England in 1942 and bought the Old Mill in Snape where Britten composed his internationally successful opera Peter Grimes with Pears playing the titular role. In 1947, Pears conceived the idea of holding a music festival in Aldeburgh, the town where they lived together.

Peter Pears and Benjamin Britten at Crag House Aldeburgh 1954. Reproduced courtesy of Britten Pears Arts. PH/3/36A.

The Aldeburgh Festival is held every year in June celebrating not only music but also poetry, drama, literature and art.

We have a comprehensive understanding of the deep bond that Britten and Pears shared from the extensive collection of letters housed in Britten Pears Arts Archive. Their love for one another was sophisticated and intensely ardent, with the letters revealing their exchanges of affection and feelings of longing when apart. The letters also demonstrate that despite the dangers of persecution by the law and the public, the two men lived together contentedly, enjoying and experiencing life the same way a married couple would.

Poster for a concert by Peter Pears and Benjamin Britten in East Bergholt. Friday 10th November 1961. 2321/7/1/3. Copyright Stour Valley Arts and Music Society.

Britten and Pears
Dr Christopher Hilton

Christopher is the Head of Archives and Library at The Red House for Britten Pears Arts.

Benjamin Britten was rooted deeply in Suffolk: born in Lowestoft in 1913, he lived most of his life in Aldeburgh and died there in 1976. His 1945 opera Peter Grimes, based on a poem by the Suffolk poet George Crabbe, made him a celebrity and revolutionised opera in the English language: in the mid-20th century he was effectively Britain's national composer, commissioned to write an opera for the Queen's coronation, and the War Requiem for the consecration of the new Coventry Cathedral. His very last published work, indeed, was written in this role as a public composer: a Welcome Ode to greet the Queen on a visit to Ipswich in her Silver Jubilee year, which Britten did not live to hear performed.

Britten's art made him a public figure, but it grew from something that made him, all his life, something of an outsider: he was a gay man at a time that this was against the law. In his twenties he met the young tenor Peter Pears and the two men formed a lifelong relationship, living together as essentially a married couple: they are buried side by side in Aldeburgh churchyard.

Britten and Pears were partners in both the professional and personal senses. Britten wrote extensively for Pears' voice: Pears had leading roles in his operas from Peter Grimes, in which he played the title character, to Britten's last opera Death in Venice; he sang the tenor part in the premiere of the War Requiem, and was the first performer of many of Britten's song cycles and other vocal pieces. Their professional partnership provided a degree of cover during the years in which male homosexuality was illegal, but their personal relationship was a very open secret: the two men had decided that they would neither flaunt nor hide their relationship, and for many years they provided Britain's best-known example of a gay couple. And in his music, Britten spoke more openly about their relationship than it was possible to do outside his art: for instance, his 1947 Canticle I set Francis Quarles' religious poem "My beloved is mine, and I am his". Whilst they retained just enough plausible deniability to stay out of trouble with the law – for example, they never had a joint bank account or held property in common - the nature of their relationship was clear to anyone who paid attention.

The Red House, their Aldeburgh home, now houses their archive. In the last years of his life, Britten expressed the hope that later biographers would tell the truth openly about his and Pears'

Bought of

O. & C. BUTCHER (OUTFITTERS) LTD.

No. 2126

B. Britten, Esq.,
"Red House,"
Golf Lane,
Aldeburgh.

129 HIGH STREET
ALDEBURGH
SUFFOLK
Telephone - 2229

1st January, 196 6.

ACCOUNTS RENDERED MONTHLY

		£	s.	d.
1965.				
28 Oct.	Shoe repairs (for Mr. Pears).		8	6
16 Dec	One Dressing Gown.	6	16	6
	One Overnight Case.	4	14	6
	Three Ties @ 9/6.	1	8	6
	One Scarf.		15	6
	One Polisher.		15	6
	One Pair of Sporting Mitts.	1	9	6
	One Pair of Hose.		9	11
	One Pair of Hose.		10	11
	One Pair of Hose.		12	6
	Two Viyella Shirts @ 69/6.	6	19	0
	Two Bow Ties @ 14/6.	1	9	0
	Four Pairs of Socks @ 12/11	2	11	8
		29	1	6

Invoice for shoe repairs from O&C Butcher, Aldeburgh. 1965. Reproduced courtesy of Britten Pears Arts. BBF/2/21/1

long relationship and celebrate how central it had been to their lives and artistic work: the archive allows us to do just that. We can see even in the most mundane papers the subterfuges that they had to undertake, but also the way they were accepted as a couple in their town: for instance, a receipt for Britten buying clothes on Aldeburgh High Street contains the line "Shoe repairs (for Mr Pears)", which tells us that Britten had to make it clear to an auditor who might see the papers that the two men were keeping their expenses separate and had no joint account, but also that the people in the shop knew that the two men lived together and were happy to put Pears' shoes on Britten's bill. And we can read the several hundred letters that the two men exchanged when apart; passionate, affectionate and, as they grow older, filled with joy as they look back on how their relationship has been so sustaining and central to their lives.

| **1951** | *Roberta Cowell is the first known British trans woman to undergo reassignment surgery and have her birth certificate changed* |

Gender dysphoria is a term that describes the distress that a person may have because their gender identity does not match the gender they were assigned at birth. This sense of dysphoria can come in three forms: physical, social and mental dysphoria. If not addressed, the distress can cause serious mental health implications. Sometimes gender dysphoria can be lessened by changing physical appearance or having gender reaffirming procedures but this is not always the case for all trans or gender non-binary people.

Gender reassignment surgery is the process of changing a person's physical sexual characteristics with an operation and/or medical procedures. Someone can undergo a gender reassignment without medical treatment by deciding to live permanently as a different gender from their biological sex or their assigned gender at birth.

Megan's Story

Megan is a trans woman living in Lowestoft. She is a trustee of Great Yarmouth and Waveney Pride committee and works in a LGBTQ+ friendly bar.

'It is a more acceptable thing these days to express your sexual and gender identity. I think 'coming out' should be a thing of the past. And there is still a way to go with equality in employment.'

'Just be yourself, people will love you more for it. And those who don't accept you aren't worth wasting time on. Don't keep putting it off for fear of other opinions and reactions.'

Barby Wire's story

Barby Wire is a drag queen who performs in Ipswich. Barby is particularly passionate about rapping and is striving to bring rap into the LGBTQ+ culture through their work. They have lived in Suffolk since they were a young child. Barby gave us an insight into the changes that have happened to the LGBTQ+ community in their lifetime and shared their thoughts on what still needs to change.

'I feel more empowered to be myself but it's still concerning. There are a lot more celebs and shows reinforcing people to become themselves and its really nice but we still see hate crimes out there and areas where there are a lot of very let's say, 'traditional' beliefs held. Although I am proud of who I am, sometimes it's hard to not care what people think. That's what can stop me. However, amongst the right people, I feel great.'

'Different is great! Don't listen to people when they criticise your fashion! You look great and you know it! Dress how you want, do what makes you happy.'

Artwork by and featuring Barby Wire.
"I have learnt to not care as much what other people think and love myself. That's what I'm trying to show."

1952 ▸ *Alan Turing convicted of 'gross indecency'*

Alan Turing was a pioneer in computing science and artificial intelligence as well as a mathematician. During the Second World War, Turing was key to cracking the German Enigma code, aiding the Allied victory over Nazi Germany.

In 1952 Turing reported a burglary of his home to the police where he informed them that he was in an active relationship with a man named Arnold Murray. Instead, the police arrested Turing and he was charged for 'gross indecency'.

Turing was given the choice between a prison sentence and chemical castration; he chose the latter. He was also barred from working for GCHQ as a result of his conviction.

The chemicals that were administered to Turing were intended to prevent his sexual urges of attraction to men.

In June 1954 Turing died of cyanide poisoning. The inquest at the time ruled his death as an act of suicide but this has been contested in recent years. In 2009 a petition began calling for the British Government to pardon Turing of his conviction gaining 30,000 signatures. A bill for Turing's pardon was brought into effect in 2014 and this led to in 2017 the eventual pardon of all people who were historically convicted of 'gross indecency'.

1954 ▸ *The Wolfenden Committee is formed after successions of well-known men are convicted of 'gross indecency', calling into question the legitimacy of the law*

In the immediate post war period convictions of 'gross indecency' increased and the Home Office pursued prosecution more rigorously.

The government set up a departmental committee under Sir John Wolfenden to consider both 'homosexual offences' and 'prostitution'. Wolfenden's report put forward the argument that homosexual behaviour between consenting adults in a private setting should no longer be a criminal offence. The recommendation explicitly stated:

'the laws of any society must be acceptable to the general moral sense of the community if they are to be respected and enforced. But we are not charged to enter into matters of private moral conduct except in so far as they directly affect the public good...'

Although the report seemed to signal a growing acceptance for same-sex relationships and acts, the vocabulary used reveals the undercurrent of disapproval with one of the chapters titled 'The Extent of the Problem'.

Despite the recommendation of the report, it was not until 1967 that homosexuality became legal in England and Wales.

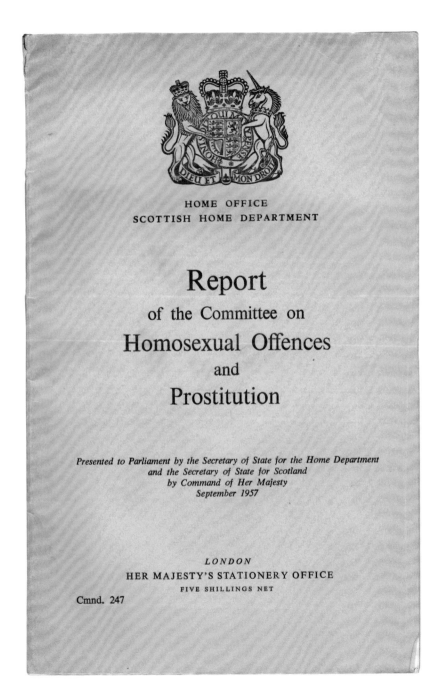

HOME OFFICE
SCOTTISH HOME DEPARTMENT

Report
of the Committee on
Homosexual Offences
and
Prostitution

*Presented to Parliament by the Secretary of State for the Home Department
and the Secretary of State for Scotland
by Command of Her Majesty
September 1957*

LONDON
HER MAJESTY'S STATIONERY OFFICE
FIVE SHILLINGS NET

Cmnd. 247

*The Wolfenden Report of the
Departmental Committee on
Homosexual Offences and
Prostitution, 1954.*

Throughout this publication, we avoided using the terms 'homosexuality' and 'homosexual' to describe people who are gay/lesbian or when referring to same-sex orientation and relationships, with the understanding that some members of the LGBTQ+ community are not comfortable with the clinical nature of these words. In certain sections, however, we decided to include these terms for the purpose of historical context and accuracy.

Queer in the Country
Timothy Allsop

How do we make rural queer experiences more visible? Timothy is an actor, writer and the co-founder of Turn of Phrase, a workshop company that focuses on gender equality through speech from Suffolk. He is spearheading the Queer Rural Connections project that explores the lives of LGBTQ+ people living in rural spaces.

For a long time, I felt the best way to make a life as a young gay man from Suffolk was to move to the city because that is where I had seen gay people, gay venues and gay culture. In the books I read and the films I saw, there was a recurring narrative of an 'escape' to the city. Didier Eribon presents the most compelling of these escape stories in *Returning to Reims*. I always yearned to return to the countryside but wondered how I would belong. The belief that rural spaces are not meant for LGBTQIA+ people persists, partly because we see such a vibrant urban queer culture, but also because not enough attention has been given to rural queer experience both current and historical. And make no mistake: there has always been a queer presence in the countryside. In a survey by the Office of National Statistics, 1.2 per cent of the East of England identified as LGB , which would translate to about 50,000 people (not including those who did not want to identify themselves). For many of us, much of our identity is located in the rural space but there also remain challenges to living in the countryside.

I remember sneaking off after my A Levels and taking a train from Stowmarket to Norwich to go to a gay pub on the edge of the city called The Castle. I ordered a pint and sat

Peter Wildblood's book *Against the Law* accounts his experiences after being prosecuted for conspiracy to incite acts of 'gross indecency'. Wildblood was a journalist for the Daily Mail as well as a former RAF pilot and meteorologist. In 1952 he was invited to the beach hut of Lord Montagu of Beaulieu with his lover Edward McNally along with Michael Pitt-Rivers. They were arrested in 1954 with Montagu, Pitt-Rivers and Wildblood being sentenced to 12 and 18 months imprisonment.

The book was the first time anyone in the English language had self-identified in print as being explicitly gay, rather than simply admitting to same-sex acts. It is considered to be an early example of a 'coming out' text and in the book he argues that not only should homosexuality be accepted by society, but that equality should be expected.

awkwardly on a stool. After a few minutes a middle-aged man came in and we started talking. I looked nervous as hell, arrogantly assuming I was being hit on, but after he had finished his drink, he wished me goodnight and left to pick up a Chinese takeaway. I didn't stay long, but on the way home, I felt a wave of excitement that I had been in a gay space talking to gay people. LGBTQIA+ spaces have been vital meeting points for the community but many of them have been forced to close, and in rural areas, where only one or two places existed, the loss can be devastating. Craig and Jon, a couple who live near Ipswich, spoke of the joy of going to both Betty's in Ipswich and the Fox and Hounds, near Manningtree. They offered space to 'build a social circle', and Jon remembers how people drove 'from miles around' to come to the Fox and Hounds. A queer space allowed them somewhere to go to socialize and forget about being in a minority for a while. Simon, the former landlord of The Wynford Arms, explained how 'the pub offered space for support groups and held fundraising events.' Social apps and high rents have made many of these social spaces unviable,

so that, while it may now be easier to meet other queer people in the countryside online, it is much harder to find a communal space.

Yet, through my research and interviews, it is clear many LGBTQIA+ people are trying to make queer life more visible in the countryside. Richard, a gardener who works on a Norfolk estate, runs the annual Rainbow Garden party, which draws 700 people from across East Anglia. Adria Pittock, who is chair of Suffolk Pride, said that over 3,000 people attended 2019's Pride events. There are also many youth organizations such as Outreach Youth, who have created social and support services for young LGBTQIA+ people living in Suffolk and Norfolk. The Pride in Suffolk's Past archive project is also a vital expression of LGBTQIA+ people reclaiming the countryside by dispelling the myth that it has been wholly heterosexual and by uncovering our collective history. Had I known in the 1990s that there had been a history of queer people living and working in the countryside, perhaps I would have been less likely to assume that being gay meant being urban.

The Stonewall Riots

On 28th June 1969, an uprising was sparked at the Stonewall Inn in New York City. The inn was a popular haunt for the LGBTQ+ community in the city and it was raided by the police in the early hours. The police were cracking down on bars which did not have Liquor Authority Licences. Many bars were refused licences because they served the LGBTQ+ community, forcing them to operate as illegal saloons, often with links to the Mafia. Officers threw out around 200 customers and began pushing customers and workers into police vehicles.

In this instance, however, the crowd turned on the police officers and violently resisted their intervention. The customers who had been ejected out on to Christopher Street attracted members of the public, increasing the number of protestors to several hundred. The next night more people gathered in protest on Christopher Street and continued to do so for another four nights. This act of resistance from the LGBTQ+ community in New York City, which was led by trans women of colour such as Storme DeLarverie and Marsha P. Johnson, is considered as the catalyst for the LGBTQ+ Equal Rights Movement. Consequently, the Gay Liberation Front (GFL) was founded and the Gay Liberation Day March of 1970 would evolve into the annual Pride marches we now know. Another organisation that emerged in the wake of the Stonewall uprising was Street Transvestite Action Revolutionaries (S.T.A.R.) - an organisation founded by Sylvia Rivera and Marsha P. Johnson in 1970.

Marsha P. Johnson and a friend at Christopher Street Liberation Day in New York City in 1976. Copyright Biscayne/Kim Peterson.

1967 *Homosexuality decriminalised in England and Wales*

The Sexual Offences Act was passed during Harold Wilson's premiership when several other liberal social reforms were also passed such as the legalisation of abortion and the lifting of censorship on the theatre. Many of the politicians who voted for decriminalisation did not necessarily condone homosexuality but did not think it should be the responsibility of the law to punish gay men for their sexual actions.

1971 *The Nullity of Marriage Act was passed*

This act explicitly banned marriages between same-sex couples in England and Wales, the first time it had been officially outlined in the law.

1972 *The first Pride is held in London, attracting approximately 2,000 participants*

The first Pride March was held on the 1st July 1972 and was organised by the Gay Liberation Front. It was organised to coincide with the anniversary of the Stonewall Riots. Along with the march, there was a rally and a picnic in Hyde Park. A small march took place the previous year with around 200 marchers with the march starting on Oxford Street and ending at Trafalgar Square.

Photograph of the first Pride March held in London in 1972. Courtesy of LSE Library

Terry Higgins was one of the first people in the UK to die of an AIDS-related illness. He was 37 when he died in July 1982 at St Thomas' Hospital. The Terrence Higgins Trust was set up by his partner Rupert Whitaker and his friend Martyn Butler with the intention of preventing other people from suffering in the same way as Terry. Their aims were to raise funds for research and raise public awareness of the illness.

The *Fightback Trust*

Prior to the late 1970s, HIV and AIDs were not widely spoken about or reported on. By 1980, however, the disease had spread to five continents including Europe and had become the subject of intense media focus.

B y 1982 it was suggested that the cause of the transmission of immune deficiency was sexual and the syndrome was initially named 'Gay-related immune deficiency' (GRID).

Referred to as the 'gay virus plague' by The Mail on Sunday in the 1980s, the reporting of the disease was rife with homophobia. Reports often, unnecessarily, dwelled upon how an individual contracted the disease, fear mongering and victim-blaming.

What are HIV and AIDS?

Human Immunodeficiency Virus (HIV) is a virus that damages the cells in the immune system and weakens a person's ability to fight everyday infections and diseases. Acquired Immune Deficiency Syndrome (AIDS) is the name used to describe a number of potentially life-threatening infections and illnesses that can happen when the immune system is severely damaged by the HIV virus. AIDS cannot be transmitted from one person to another, but HIV can.

There is no cure for HIV but there are now effective drug treatments that enable most people with the virus to live a long life. Accurate information is the best antidote to the fear and stigma that comes with HIV. ACT UP NY lists several ways in which transmition of HIV can be prevented: taking Pre-Exposure Prophylaxis, a daily medication to immunise against infection (known as PrEP), taking Post Exposure Prophylaxis (PEP) for 28 days after being exposed to the virus, and fighting existing infections so that you are no longer able to infect others (known as U=U). The most common way the virus is transmitted is through sexual intercourse without a condom but can also be transmitted through sharing needles and from mother to baby.

This homophobic reporting only made it harder for victims to come forward and seek help. In order to protect against the disease, conversations needed to be had and the stigma needed to be ended. These were exactly the aims of the Fightback charity in Lowestoft. The founders of the charity Bryn Morris and Adrian Strickland wanted to make sure that their experiences were never repeated.

Speaking to the Lowestoft Journal in 1992 the aims of Fightback were to remove the hype surrounding HIV and AIDS, improve the awareness, and to 'make the community as safe as possible for future generations.' The article celebrates the opening of a new HIV and AIDs resource centre, the first of its kind in Suffolk. It offered up-to-date, accurate information, a drop-in facility, private counselling, and a telephone helpline that covered Norwich, Ipswich, Bury St Edmunds, Yarmouth, and Lowestoft.

Photograph from the launch of the Fightback trust in 1992. 1176/1/15/3/6/3 Archant Library/EADT

1988 ▸ Section 28 of the Local Government Act

Section 28 was part of a law passed in May 1988 which banned councils and schools from 'the promotion of homosexuality by local authorities'. The children's book *Jenny Lives with Eric and Martin* was published in 1983 with the aim of teaching children about different family relationships. This received criticism from Prime Minister Margaret Thatcher who believed that children needed to respect 'traditional moral values'.

As a result of Section 28, many children and young people who were coming to terms with their sexuality or gender did not receive support from schools as staff were prohibited from promoting the acceptability of same-sex relationships. The law was not fully repealed until 2003.

1989 ▸ Stonewall UK was founded

A small group of people who were struggling against Section 28 founded the Stonewall UK to campaign and lobby against attacks on LGBTQ+ people. Over the years they have had an integral role in lifting the ban on Lesbian, Gay and Bisexual people serving in the military and making the age of consent equal for same-sex relations as well as repealing Section 28. They continue to work on behalf of LGBTQ+ people in the UK today.

An anonymous story

An anonymous contributor told us about the difficulties they had coming out in the 1980s during the AIDS Pandemic.

'I was spat at, beaten and insulted. Teachers turned a blind eye, as did family and "friends". I was never the most confident person anyway, so this really dragged me right down.

People looked at you like something on their shoe, crossing the street to avoid me "in case they catch AIDS" or become gay because I speak to them.'

Yet they are glad that positive changes have been made in recent years:

'I was so pleased when same sex marriage was allowed. However, we still have so far to go. Equal in law but not society is my way of describing it.'

It was initially added classified in 1977 but was removed from the International Classification of Diseases in 1990.

Clare's story

Clare and her wife on their wedding day in 2015.

Clare and her now wife aged 19 and 21 in 1986 just before they got thrown out of a Norwich pub for kissing each other.

'I have been lucky. I've experienced very little direct abuse. The worst was back in 1986/7 when my then lover and I were publicly humiliated and thrown out of a pub in Norwich after the landlady saw us kissing in the beer garden. It was terrible at the time.

I 'ran away' from my first love at Uni in 1986. I was scared (because of Section 28 and being a trainee teacher and all that). I subsequently married a man - my parents were delighted. He turned out to be violent & abusive. I was 27 when I came out.

The woman I met at 19 (she was 21) with whom I was thrown out of a pub for kissing in 1986 and didn't see for nearly 30 years, is now my wife of 5 years. We live in Suffolk with our 17-year-old daughter very happily.'

Supporting young LGBT*Q+ people in Suffolk

Andy Fell

Outreach youth is a LGBT*Q+ youth work charity based in Ipswich, working with and providing support to young LGBT*Q+ people and their families. Andy is the LGBT*Q+ Youth Development worker for Outreach Youth.

Established in 2006, the charity has developed its services for young people – currently providing LGBT*Q+ youth groups, One to One support, Trans* Families groups, Targeted Youth work, Social Action projects, Advocacy, Youth Led Events and Education sessions for schools, colleges and professionals.

The charity is committed to the youth principles of Education, Equality, Empowerment and Participation – co-producing projects and sessions with young LGBT*Q+ people.

These core values summarise our approach and ethos as a youth work organisation:

- **Positive Relationships** – we like young LGBTQ+ people and we work to build positive, respectful, appropriate and empowering relationships with young people, their families, colleagues and other professionals.
- **Respect** – we respect the young LGBTQ+ people, their families, colleagues and the professionals we work with.
- **Innovation** – we are proud that we provide innovative and high-quality youth work to young LGBTQ+ people, with a track record of providing creative solutions and looking for new ways to solving problems.
- **Integrity** – as a youth work charity we aim to be accountable and transparent to the young LGBTQ+ people we work with, our supporters and funders.
- **Aspirational** – we see youth work as being able to inspire young LGBTQ+ people and assist them to fulfil their potential – through positive and supportive youth work experiences – we aim to empower young LGBTQ+ people to build brighter futures.

One of the young people who was part of Outreach Youth's Trans Families Support Group shared their experience:

Luca, 16.

Luca began attending Trans* Families six months ago. Having come out as Trans* two years previously, Luca had had a very difficult and isolated existence in these two years before joining the project. Luca's mum was supportive but really struggled to understand and come to terms with Luca's changing identity. Luca said:

"[The project] made me feel much more comfortable and open about being trans*; the group provided me with a safe space to be honest. The group are so good at listening to each other. Being part of this group and meeting others has greatly increased my confidence, which has enabled me to move on from the group and enter the world of work as a confident and assured person. The more I went, the more confident I felt."

"I found it incredibly difficult to find information that was helpful online and there is lots of misleading information out there. Without Trans* Families and my friendship group here, the education I received would have been lacking and I would have been far more defensive on Trans* issues. The youth work approach at Outreach youth has enabled be to feel welcomed and safe to learn more about myself."

"It's given me the confidence to share who I am; I feel empowered to be me and use my voice. It's a really difficult issue and now I feel I can explain Trans* related issues to anyone and the team at Outreach youth have taught me how to be confident and assured [in doing] this,"

"The families element of the project is essential; my mum didn't understand it at first. She was open and coming to the group meeting other parents with the same struggles was very valuable to her and she now understands the importance of pronouns which is so helpful."

The Pride in Suffolk's Past project collaborated with the young people at Outreach Youth to make creative content for the exhibition in the Hold.

1999 ▸ *The Admiral Duncan Pub Attack*

On the 30th April, The Admiral Duncan, one of London's oldest gay pubs, was the target of a nail bomb attack which killed three people and seriously injured many. It was part of a series of hate crimes targeted at the Black, Bangladeshi, and LGBTQ+ communities in London. Tom Worlledge, Proprietor of The Dooley Inn pub in Felixstowe, sadly lost his son in the attack and now kindly raises funds for Suffolk Pride.

2001 ▸ *The age of consent for gay/bisexual men is lowered to 16*

In 1994 the age of consent was lowered to 18. When the age of consent was lowered to 16, it came into line with the age of consent for straight people.

Same sex couples and unmarried straight couples were now able to adopt or foster children.

Before these regulations were put into place, places of work did not provide full protection from bullying, unfair workplace rules and restrictions to being hired or promoted at work.

Miles' story

Miles is a Suffolk resident who identifies as a non-binary queer person. They were born in Ipswich and lived there until their early twenties and now live in Stowmarket. Miles gave us an insight into their life and experiences during lockdown.

‚As far as I know, I was the first non-binary queer member of Ipswich and District Trade Union Council (possibly first out LGBTQ+ member) in the late noughties and the first non-binary member of Stowmarket Town Council from 2015. I stood in district elections so Mid Suffolk District Council had at least a non-binary candidate in 2015 and 2019 if not before. I also helped set up ShOUT,

an under 30s group for LGBTQIA+ people as a volunteer at Suffolk LGB&T Network in 2012.

During lockdown, people you saw outside walking were with people from the same household. This meant there was less friends walking together and so we noticed other queer couples more.

Not having to worry about transphobia on my way to work and the wonderful warm weather meant I was able to be much more varied in work clothes and be more visibly nonbinary to neighbours.

I have also been more visibly nonbinary on zoom also due to pronouns being shown with my name, like with email signatures. This is better than in-person meetings where pronouns are often not visible.'

Working in the NHS
Nicola Cottington

Nicola is the Deputy Chief Operating Officer at James Paget University Hospitals Trust. Nicola and her wife Lorraine are the mothers to two sons and are advocates for same-sex adoption.

I qualified as a nurse in 1999 and have worked in the NHS ever since, in acute hospitals, community services and prison healthcare. I have gradually taken on more senior management roles as my career as progressed.

I experienced homophobia myself on a placement while I was a student nurse, so I understood that it's not always easy for staff to be true to themselves at work. I am generally quiet "out" at work, but even so people often make assumptions, asking what my husband does for a living. It sometimes feels like I am coming out every day.

When I was working at West Suffolk Foundation Trust, I helped set up the LGB&T+ network in 2018, the first of its kind at the Trust. I started off just going along to a workshop one of the deputy directors of HR held, for anyone interested in joining a network and I tried at first to just be a participant. I am a lesbian and I had not worked at the Trust long. I was really impressed that the organisation was looking at diversity issues and trying to set up a network. Because I manage in my day job, I thought in this situation I could just be a member and support other people to lead. However, I realised that I myself had a privilege due to my relatively senior status - I knew how to chair a meeting, book rooms and had access to Executives, and I became the chair of the network.

One of our first ambitions was to raise the visibility of LGB&T+ issues. We ordered rainbow lanyards and badge

NHS rainbow badges. Photo: Shropshire Star.

2004 ▸ Civil Partnership Act is passed

Civil partnerships were introduced to give same-sex couples the same legal rights as married couples. In 2013, the Marriage Act was passed giving same-sex couples the opportunity to get married like any other couple or convert their civil partnership to a marriage.

The BBC reported that on the day in which The Civil Partnerships Act was enacted, fourteen couples from Suffolk became civil partners.

2004 ▸ Gender Recognition Act is passed

The Gender Recognition Act gave trans people the right to legally change their gender by receiving a new birth certificate that matches their gender identity.

clips, and then I discovered the Rainbow NHS Badge project, started by Dr Michael Farquhar at the Evelina Children's Hospital in London. NHS staff wear the badge to signal they are open and welcoming to people of all genders and sexualities. We designed our own version of the pledge and ran stalls in the staff restaurant to launch the Rainbow NHS Badge in the Trust, during Pride week 2019. It was a real success and people were mostly positive. One physiotherapist came up to me in WHSmith in the hospital and told me how an elderly patient had felt able to be open to her about her sexuality (the patient was a lesbian) because she saw the rainbow. It was relevant to her clinical care as the patient was practicing transferring into her bed before she was discharged home. This is what it is all about- being explicit and intentional about

celebrating and valuing LGB&T+ people and understanding that your gender and sexuality are part of who you are. It is not enough just to "tolerate" us - LGB&T+ people have higher rates of mental and physical illness than heterosexual people, because of the homophobia and transphobia in society.

The LGB&T+ network undertook a series of events during Pride week and the rest of the year. We promoted transgender awareness training, arranged for profiles of members of the network to be included in the staff newsletter and joined up with the library to celebrate LGBT History Month. I have now started working at James Paget University Hospitals Trust, where I have just started planning how to set up an LGB&T+ network as part of the inclusion work the Trust is undertaking.

The event had support from Suffolk County Council's LGB&T Network, Suffolk Constabulary and the Suffolk Gay and Lesbian Helpline. The event took place on the 40th Anniversary year of the Stonewall Riots. The day featured stalls, live music and even an audio link-up with the Stonewall Inn in New York.

A Recent History of Suffolk Pride

Adria Pittock

Adria is the Chair of both the Suffolk Pride Committee and the Suffolk County Council staff LGBT+ Network.

Suffolk Pride came out of the shadows in June 2019 - exactly 50 years after the Stonewall riots in New York on 28th June 1969. This riot started when a group of queer people (lesbian, gay, trans, bi) fought back when the New York Police Department raided their lesbian and gay bar yet again. The movement was led by lesbians and trans women of colour. They were Marsha P. Johnson, Sylvia Rivera, and Stormé DeLarverie.

Every year since then in the Pride Month of June there have been Pride events in an increasing number of cities and towns all over the world. These are events and parades to celebrate the LGBTQ+ community and their allies and to remind people that Pride is still a protest.

There had been Pride events in Ipswich before. I think I went to my first Suffolk Pride in Christchurch Park in around 2009 and a couple since then but they have not happened on a regular basis. I give thanks to all who made these Pride events possible. They were an important part of 'growing' Pride in Suffolk and paved the way for where we are now.

In 2014, for the first time Suffolk Pride arranged a parade along the waterfront which was a great achievement, with an estimated 2,000 people; but then there was no Pride in Suffolk for 5 years until Suffolk Pride in 2019. In 2019 we closed the whole of the Waterfront and had a Parade of over 4,000 people. Suffolk Pride had "come of age"! In 2020 we had to take Suffolk Pride online and into a virtual space, which we did very successfully. Already Suffolk Pride has started planning for a combined "real" Pride on the Waterfront and "virtual" Suffolk Pride in 2021.

When I became Chair of Suffolk Pride in 2019, we decided that we needed to make Suffolk really stand up and take notice of Pride and to recognise that we had a thriving and significant LGBTQ+ community right here. We also wanted to put Pride on the map and make sure it became an established annual event in Suffolk for as long as we feel we need it.

So, we partnered with the Suffolk Food and Drink Festival on the Waterfront in Ipswich on 22nd June 2019 combining with the Suffolk Big Weekender event, when BBC Radio Suffolk shines a spotlight on all things Suffolk! The parade started at 12 o'clock and just grew and grew! Many people were coming to the Waterfront for the Food and Drink festival and they had no idea what Pride was, but they all simply joined in, there were families and young and old, the atmosphere was amazing.

People reported that Suffolk really "came together". In the end over 4,000 people "paraded" along the waterfront in support of the LGBTQ+ community of Suffolk, enjoying the food and drink stalls at Orwell Quay and the bands that Suffolk Pride put on the main stage. There was also a poetry and spoken word event, stalls and stands

Adria (right) at Suffolk Pride 2019.

showcasing products and services for the LGBTQ+ community, and we had an amazing drag afterparty at the Cult Bar.

In 2020 during our Virtual Suffolk Pride event on 27th June we were determined to have a parade and so we started with a Suffolk Pride "Parade from Home" video which over 50 people and organisations had contributed to – this has been viewed over 2,300 times on Facebook. During the day we had nearly 2,000 people dropping in on the virtual event that consisted of music, spoken word, drag, dance and other performances, plus a voguing workshop and a panel discussion. The Afterparty DJ sets gained a unique viewing total of over 8,000 people. So, Suffolk Pride online was easily as much a success as Suffolk Pride on the Waterfront and because it was not limited by geography it was accessible to more people from across Suffolk and even further afield.

In 2021 we are looking to build on our success both on the Waterfront and in the Virtual sphere and are hoping we can offer both!

2010 ▸ *The Equality Act*

This act ensures that regardless of age, sexuality, gender, disability, race, or religious belief everyone should have equal treatment and access to public and private services.

2020 ▸ *Northern Ireland legalises same-sex marriage*

It was not until January 2020 that same-sex couples were able to register to marry or have their union recognised by law in Northern Ireland. Those who have a civil partnership, however, are presently unable to convert to a marriage (as of September 2020).

Suffolk Virtual Pride

In spring 2020, during pandemic lockdown, the organisers of Suffolk Pride took the difficult but necessary decision to cancel the planned in-person Pride event on the Ipswich Waterfront that summer. However, they had no intention of letting the year pass by without marking the occasion somehow, and decided to transform the event into a Virtual Pride so that as many people could celebrate online as possible.

The organisers worked with DanceEast to create a Parade From Home video - a wonderful way to see the support the LGBTQIA+ community has from the wider community in Suffolk and beyond! The Parade also showcased LGBTQIA+ people being unapologetically proud and visible and living their best lives, something we always need more of.

The virtual event also held panel discussions with local groups and charities such as Suffolk Mind, Terrence Higgins Trust Suffolk, and Outreach Youth to chat about pressing issues that the community (still) faces today, such as inclusive sex & relationships education, reform of the Gender Recognition Act and the intersection of LGBTQ+ identities and mental health, plus their aim to make Suffolk Pride more inclusive.

The continuation of Suffolk Pride to a virtual platform gave the event huge accessibility - it helped to establish more working relationships with local organisations and groups but most importantly it reached the LGBTQ+ family on an even wider scale (including those who may not have been able to access the waterfront event previously) to celebrate themselves!

There's no denying that the event was a big undertaking, but the organisers agree that the virtual event helped them to see how vital accessibility is and going forward they would like to repeat a virtual pride in 2021 alongside the usual Suffolk Pride on the waterfront - with the view to examine how virtual fundraisers could also fit into their plans in the future.

Resources and local organisations

Please note these details were correct at the time of publication and may be subject to change.

◖ Mermaids

Help and support for transgender young people and their families.

www.mermaidsuk.org.uk

◖ Outreach Youth

Providing support for LBGTQ+ people under 25 and their families across Suffolk.

www.outreachyouth.org.uk

◖ Sam's Coffee House

LGBTQ+ Support group that meets in Lowestoft.

www.samscoffeehouse.com

◖ Samaritans

Charity providing emotional support to anyone in emotional distress, struggling to cope, or at risk of suicide. Telephone support line available 24 hours a day, 365 days a year.

www.samaritans.org 116 123

● Stonewall

Help and advice for LGBT people and their allies.
www.stonewall.org.uk/help-and-advice

● Suffolk Gender Identity Hub

Information for people who are transgender or questioning their gender identity, and for people who support them.
www.healthysuffolk.org.uk/advice-services/adults/transgender-hub

● Switchboard LGBT Helpline

Switchboard provide an information, support and referral service for LGBT people (and family and friends), and anyone considering issues around their sexuality and/or gender identity. They run a telephone service, live chat, and email.
www.switchboard.lgbt/help
0300 330 0630 Open 10am-10pm everyday

● Suffolk LGBTQ Forum

Founded in 1988. Provide support to people over 16 and a range of activities.
www.suffolklgbtnetwork.org.uk

● Suffolk Night Owls

A telephone, text, and email support service run by Suffolk Mind. Telephone details are provided once registered with the service.
www.suffolkmind.org.uk/services/suffolk-night-owls-telephone-support-line

● The Source

Help and support for young people.
www.thesource.me.uk/search-for-help-support-and-services/sexuality

Terminology

LGBTQ+	We have decided to use the acronym LGBTQ+ in our publication and exhibition. It has been used consistently in all of the content written directly by Suffolk Archives. Some contributors may have decided to use a variation of the acronym in their text. We have decided not to change these to respect the author's personal preference.
'buggery'/ 'sodomy'/ 'gross indecency'	We do not condone the use of these terms to describe same-sex acts in a contemporary context. However, we have decided to include these terms in the publication when referring to historical information, especially in reference to legal history. These words have been put into inverted commas to denote this. We also thought it important to explain the etymology of these terms so that our readers understand why they are unacceptable and derogatory in our modern vocabulary.
homosexual/ homosexuality	Throughout the publication, we have not used the terms 'homosexual' or 'homosexuality' to describe people who are gay or lesbian or when referring to same-sex orientation and relationships, with the understanding that some members of the LGBTQ+ community are not comfortable with the clinical nature of these words. In certain sections, however, we decided to include these terms for the purpose of historical context and accuracy, particularly in reference to legal changes.
same-sex marriage vs gay marriage	When referring to the Civil partnership and Marriage act, we have made sure to use the term 'same-sex marriage' rather than 'gay marriage' with the understanding that it is more inclusive. Some of our contributors, however, have used the term 'gay marriage' instead.

loving relationship vs sexual relationship	For many of the historic figures featured in the publication, we have tried to be sensitive about how we describe the relationships they had. We did not want to presume anyone's sexuality or make presumptions that a relationship was of a sexual nature. Therefore, we have sometimes used phrases such as 'romantic' 'loving' or 'passionate' to best describe our understanding of each relationship.
homophobia, transphobia and LGBTQ+ discrimination	If any form of discrimination against LGBTQ+ is discussed in the publication, we have made sure that the most accurate term has been used to describe it. E.g. not using 'homophobia' if the example includes discrimination against trans people as well.
queer	We decided not to use the term 'queer' to describe anyone in the LGBTQ+ community in any of the text directly written by Suffolk Archives, with the understanding that some members of the community find it derogatory. However, some contributors felt comfortable using this term in their contributions or have used it to self-describe their identity.
lesbian and gay woman	We decided to use the term 'lesbian' in Suffolk Archives' text as we think it best to use a word that does not define women in context to a term traditionally used to describe male same-sex relationships. However, one of our contributors self-describes as a 'gay woman'.
trans as a descriptor	We decided to use 'trans' rather than 'transgender' when describing e.g. trans people, trans history etc.
sexuality and sexual acts in context of the law	When discussing laws from the past, we have made sure to make the distinction that some laws did not directly prohibit certain sexualities but specifically sexual acts between people of the same sex. However, we acknowledge that as a consequence, people of certain sexualities or gender identity were persecuted.
Pride vs Gay Pride	We decided to use 'Pride' instead of 'Gay Pride' when referring any form of pride march or celebration to be fully inclusive of the whole LGBTQ+ community who celebrate pride. However, we acknowledge in the publication that the first pride march was organised by the Gay Liberation Front.

Acknowledgements

Thank you to all who have supported the development of the Pride in Suffolk's Past publication:

- The Suffolk Pride committee for their consultation and support

- The Suffolk County Council LGBT+ staff network for their consultation and advice

- Suffolk Archives Volunteers

- All of the contributors who wrote pieces for the book: Dr Louise Carter, Zelly Lisanework, Christopher Hilton, Timothy Allsop, Andy Fell, Nicola Cottington and Adria Pittock.

- All those who contributed to the Pride in Suffolk's Past collecting online survey.

- Thanks to the following organisations and individuals who contributed images: Zelly Lisanework, Peter Bance, Bury Past and Present Society, Georgia Goddard, The Women's Library at LSE, Mary Evans Picture Library, National Portrait Gallery, Britten Pears Arts, Barby Wire, Megan, Biscayne/Kim Peterson, LSE Library, Archant, Clare, Cherry Wizz Fizz Design, Adria Pittock and Suffolk Pride.

Pride in Suffolk's Past is a Sharing Suffolk's Stories project funded and supported by the National Lottery Heritage Fund, the University of Suffolk, Suffolk County Council, and the Coastal Communities Fund.